The
Enchanting
World

Coloring Book

The Enchanting World

Coloring Book

Magical designs to charm and inspire

SIRIUS

SIRIUS

This edition published in 2023 by Sirius Publishing, a division of
Arcturus Publishing Limited,
26/27 Bickels Yard, 151–153 Bermondsey Street,
London SE1 3HA

ISBN: 978-1-3988-3155-1
CH011122NT
Supplier 29, Date 0423, PI 00003294

Printed in China

Introduction

A world of magic awaits you within the pages of this coloring book. You'll find all kinds of fantastical beings, including dragons, unicorns, and super-sized eagles, large enough to bear a human in flight. There are fairies that appear as flowers—and friendly elves—as well as trolls fearsome enough to terrorize a whole kingdom. And we've conjured a host of magical realms, from the tiny toadstool houses that might be occupied by a fairy, to castles that sit atop a whole fantastical world. And there are many ways to enter them, including keys, magic mirrors, or special potions that can enlarge or reduce the drinker. If you want to lose yourself in these special places, find your own quiet place, choose a magical image to color, and select pencils in the hues you want to use. Then while away an hour or two creating your own magic.

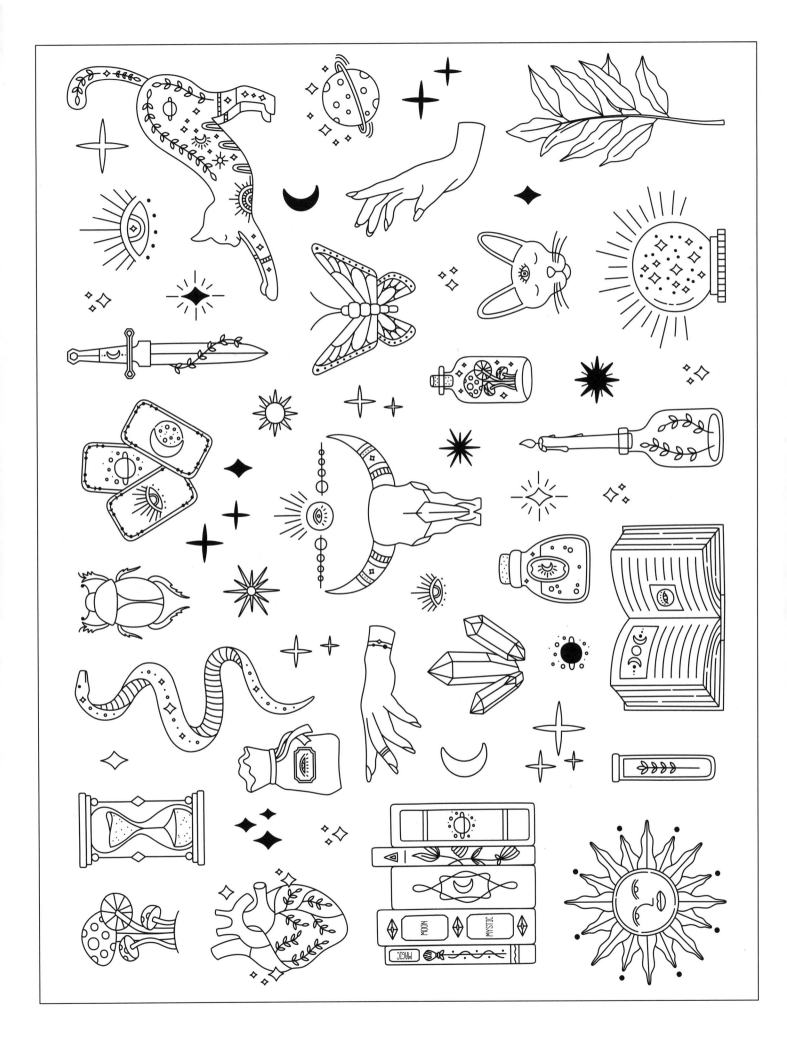

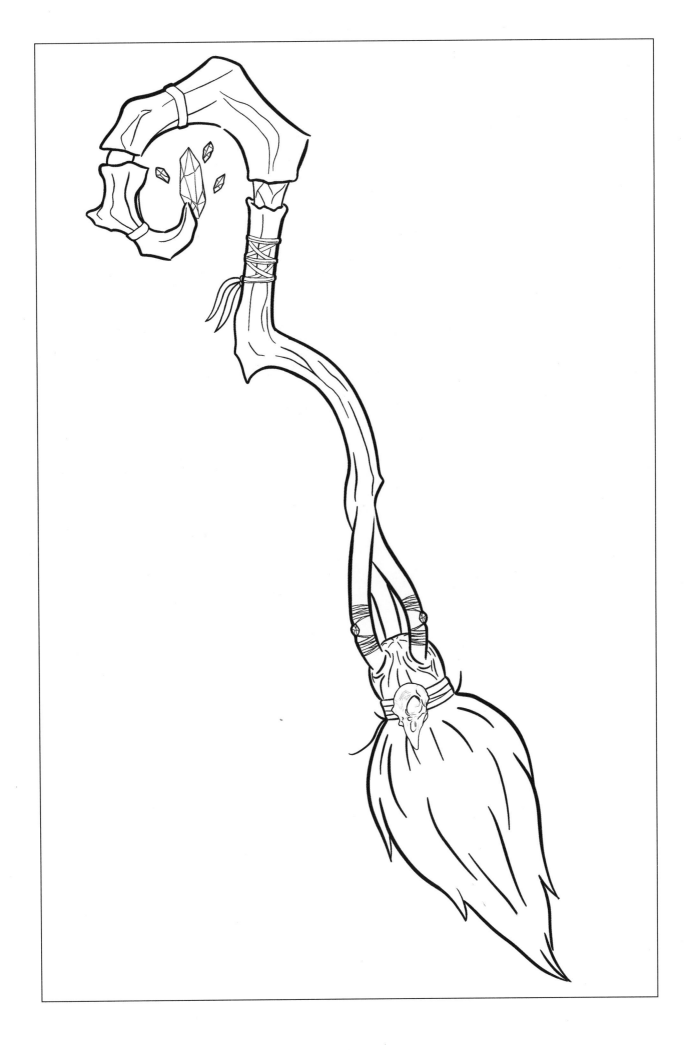

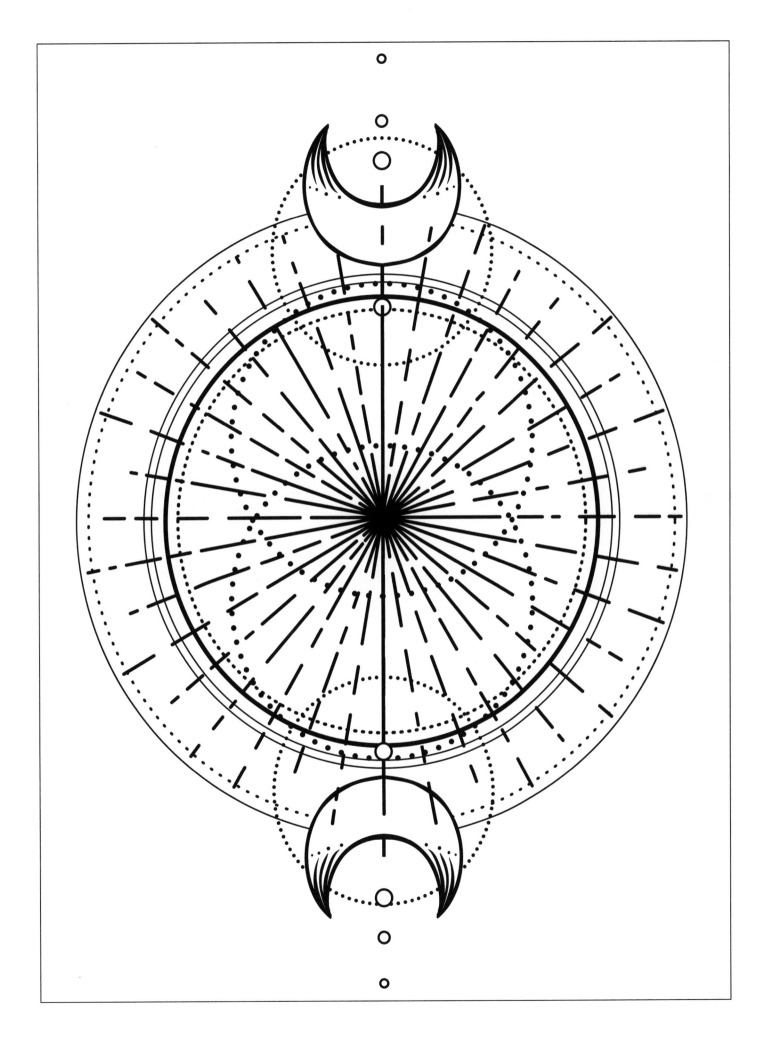

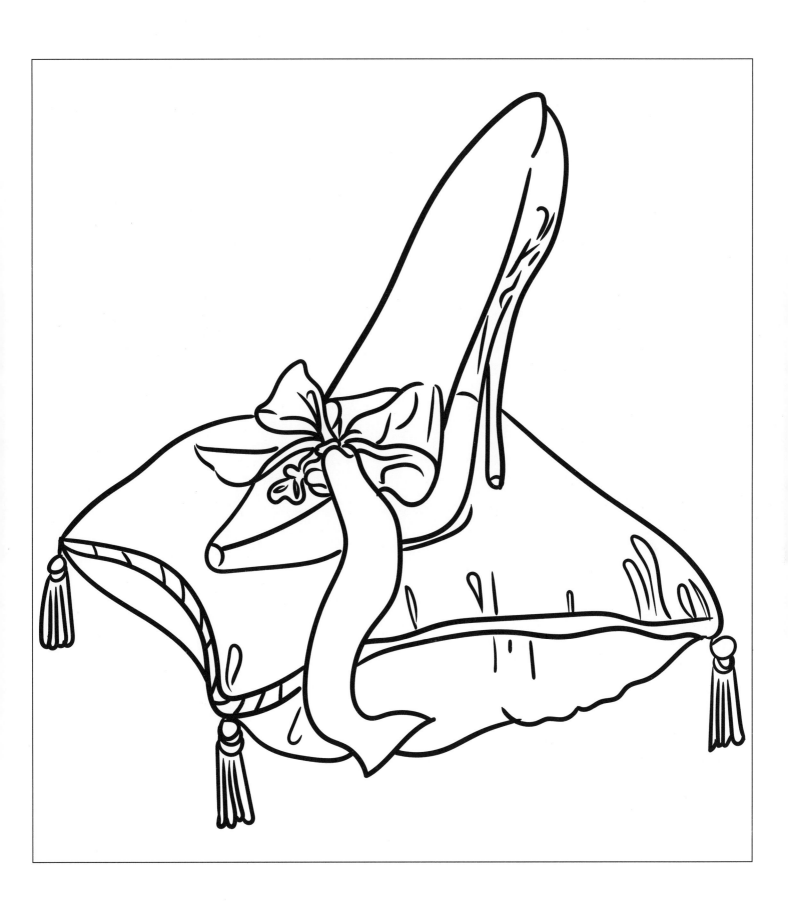